Advanced Cybersecurity Tools & Strategies

Encryption, Firewalls, Secure Cloud Storage, Threat Detection & Incident Response for Non-Techies

By Joe Correa

Published by Live Stronger Faster

First Edition

Table of Contents

Introduction

In an era where cyberattacks happen every 39 seconds, and data breaches impact millions without warning, the conversation around digital safety can no longer be limited to IT professionals. Today, everyone—entrepreneurs, freelancers, parents, students, even retirees—needs to understand more than just the basics of cybersecurity. It's no longer just about installing antivirus software and creating strong passwords. The threats are evolving, and so must your defenses.

That's where this book comes in.

Advanced Cybersecurity Tools & Strategies was created for people who've already been introduced to cybersecurity fundamentals and want to take their protection to the next level—without becoming a full-time hacker or hiring a tech team. If you've read the earlier books in this series, you've learned how to spot phishing scams, use privacy settings, and secure your mobile devices. Now it's time to dig deeper. Encryption, firewalls, cloud security, threat detection, and response planning are the real-world tools used by cyber experts, and they're no longer optional. They're essential—and surprisingly, you don't need a tech background to use them effectively.

This isn't a book about hacking or coding. It's about helping you build a fortress around your digital life using powerful but accessible tools. You'll learn how encryption protects your emails and files from prying eyes, how different types of firewalls act as your first line of defense, and how to choose cloud storage that keeps your sensitive documents safe. We'll also explore antivirus systems and threat detection tools, showing you how they work and when they fail. And because no system is perfect, we'll finish with a crash course in creating your own incident response plan—so you'll know exactly what to do when something goes wrong.

You may be wondering: "Do I really need this level of protection?" The answer is simple. If you own a smartphone, manage client data, send private messages, shop online, or store anything sensitive in the cloud, the answer is yes. Cybersecurity isn't just about keeping hackers out—it's about preserving your freedom, reputation, finances, and peace of mind.

What makes this book different is the focus on simplicity and action. Every strategy you'll read here has been carefully chosen for non-tech users—people like you, who want results without the jargon. I'll break things down step by step and share real-life scenarios where these tools saved businesses, protected personal files, or helped recover from an attack. You don't need to be "good with computers" to build a strong security system—you just need the right roadmap. That's what this book is.

Throughout the chapters, you'll find tool recommendations, setup tips, and warning signs to look out for. You'll also learn how to layer your defenses, a concept known as defense-in-depth, which dramatically increases your odds of staying safe even if one system fails. This layered approach is the gold standard in cybersecurity, and you'll be amazed at how easy it can be to apply with the right guidance.

By the end of this book, you won't just have better tools—you'll have confidence. Confidence that your files are encrypted, that your devices are being monitored, that your cloud storage is secure, and that you have a clear action plan for any cyber incident. You'll know which tools are worth paying for and which ones you can get for free. You'll be empowered to make smarter decisions about the apps you use, the emails you open, and the networks you connect to.

Cybersecurity is no longer optional. But becoming cyber-proficient doesn't have to be complicated, expensive, or stressful. With the right knowledge, you can protect yourself and your business from most modern digital threats—and you can do it starting today.

So, if you're ready to go from passive user to proactive defender—without learning how to code—let's begin.

Chapter 1: Why "Advanced" Doesn't Mean "Complicated"

Jasmine Hernandez ran a six-figure online marketing consultancy from her laptop. Her days were packed with virtual meetings, email campaigns, and client onboarding forms—all of which relied on sensitive client information being securely stored and transmitted. She thought she was careful: strong passwords, a paid antivirus software, and a VPN for public Wi-Fi. But Jasmine was about to learn that digital threats don't wait for you to be tech-savvy. They simply look for the next weak link.

It started on a regular Tuesday. Jasmine had just wrapped up a webinar and clicked on what looked like a routine Dropbox file shared by a returning client. Within minutes, her screen froze. Then her files vanished. Pop-ups began appearing, demanding Bitcoin in exchange for unlocking her system. She'd been hit by ransomware. A faceless attacker had gained access to her files and encrypted everything—her business contracts, tax records, client databases—gone.

Panicked, she called her friend Marcus, an IT consultant. After hearing the symptoms, he asked, "Do you have endpoint detection software? A firewall? Secure cloud backups?"

"No... I have antivirus and I use iCloud," she replied, still shaking.

Marcus sighed. "Antivirus helps with viruses, but ransomware and today's attacks are more complex. You need layered protection—firewalls, encryption, real cloud backups with versioning, and some form of detection."

In the days that followed, Jasmine learned more about cybersecurity than she ever wanted to know. But oddly, it wasn't as complicated as she feared. With Marcus's help, she rebuilt her system: installed a hardware firewall at home, subscribed to secure cloud storage with automatic backups, enabled full-disk encryption, and replaced her single antivirus software with an endpoint protection suite that monitored unusual behavior. She even created an incident response playbook—a simple checklist that told her what to do in case of another cyberattack.

Weeks later, she reflected on what had happened. Jasmine hadn't been careless—she'd just believed that "basic" protection was enough. But in a world where cybercriminals deploy AI and automation to scale their attacks, basic is now outdated. What she learned, and what she now shared with clients, is that advanced tools don't require an advanced degree. They just require awareness and action.

That experience changed Jasmine's business. Not only did she implement better security, but she added digital risk assessments as part of her consulting packages. What once seemed like a weakness had become a value-add. And as she told her clients: "You don't need to be a tech expert. You just need the right system, the right mindset, and a bit of guidance. Because today, advanced cybersecurity is just smart business."

Chapter 2: Encryption: Securing Your Emails, Files, and Devices

Encryption is often viewed as some mysterious, high-level tool only used by spies and tech giants. But in reality, it's one of the simplest, most effective ways to secure your information—and it's available to everyone. In this chapter, we'll break down what encryption is, how it works, where it should be applied in your life, and what tools you can start using right now.

Let's start with the basics. Encryption is the process of converting information into a coded format so that only someone with the correct key can access it. Think of it as putting your data into a locked safe. Even if someone steals the safe, they can't open it without the right combination. Modern encryption uses mathematical algorithms that are practically impossible to break without the decryption key, making it a top-tier security solution.

There are two main types of encryption: **symmetric** and **asymmetric**. Symmetric encryption uses the same key to encrypt and decrypt data. It's fast and efficient, perfect for internal systems or encrypted hard drives. Asymmetric encryption, on the other hand, uses a public key to encrypt data and a private key to decrypt it. This method is common in email encryption, secure messaging, and digital signatures.

You've likely used it without realizing it every time you visit a website with "https" in the address bar.

So, where should you use encryption in your daily life or business? Start with your devices. Enable **full-disk encryption** on your laptop and phone. On Macs, it's called FileVault; on Windows, it's BitLocker. These tools encrypt everything on your hard drive, protecting your data even if your device is stolen. For mobile devices, most newer models automatically encrypt data, but you should still check that encryption is turned on in your settings.

Next, consider encrypting your emails—especially if you're sharing contracts, client details, or anything sensitive. Tools like ProtonMail, Tutanota, or extensions like Mailvelope allow you to send encrypted messages that only your recipient can read. For messaging apps, Signal and WhatsApp use end-to-end encryption by default, which means not even the app provider can read your messages.

Don't forget your cloud storage. Many popular platforms like Dropbox, Google Drive, and iCloud encrypt data in transit (while it's being uploaded) and at rest (while it's stored). However, the service provider often holds the encryption keys, which means they could potentially access your files. For added control, use zero-knowledge cloud services like

Sync.com, pCloud, or Tresorit—these ensure that only you have access to the encryption keys.

File-level encryption is another step you can take. Tools like VeraCrypt or AxCrypt let you encrypt specific files or folders before uploading them to the cloud. This adds a strong extra layer of protection, particularly for sensitive documents like tax returns, contracts, or personal ID scans.

Finally, understand the importance of key management. Encryption is only as secure as the place you store your keys. Never email your decryption key alongside the encrypted file. Use a password manager to store your encryption keys or recovery phrases securely. If you're using services with multi-factor authentication (which you should be), make sure your recovery codes are also protected.

Encryption may sound intimidating, but once you understand the logic and have the right tools in place, it becomes second nature. You don't need to encrypt everything—just the things that matter most. Think of it as a seatbelt for your digital life. You hope you never need it, but when something goes wrong, it can be the difference between a small scare and a total disaster.

The story of encryption

Tommy was a freelance tax advisor who worked remotely with dozens of clients across the U.S. His business was growing fast, and he prided himself on being reliable, responsive, and discreet. But when a new client insisted on using ProtonMail for all communication, Tommy was caught off guard.

"Why don't we just use Gmail?" he asked.

"Because I'm sending you W-2s, bank statements, and social security numbers. If that gets intercepted, I lose everything," the client replied bluntly.

That night, Tommy did some research. He discovered that while Gmail encrypts messages during transmission, Google still had access to them. And if someone hacked his account, they'd have full access too. He signed up for ProtonMail the same night.

A few weeks later, Tommy's phone was stolen while traveling. At first, he panicked—what about the client messages? The personal files? Then he remembered that his phone was encrypted, protected with a passcode and remote wipe capability. He logged into his laptop, used the device manager to erase the phone remotely, and exhaled for the first time in hours.

From that moment on, Tommy became obsessed with encryption. He enabled FileVault on his MacBook, used Signal for messaging, stored client documents in a zero-knowledge cloud platform, and encrypted every tax return before sending it out. He even created a one-page cheat sheet for his clients explaining how to open encrypted files securely.

Clients noticed. They trusted him more, recommended him more, and one even said, "You're the only person I trust with my finances outside my CPA." What began as a reluctant adjustment turned into a unique value proposition. In a field where privacy was everything, Tommy's use of encryption became a business advantage.

Encryption didn't just protect Tommy's business—it elevated it. And it all started with a single client who refused to settle for "convenient."

Chapter 3: Firewalls 101: What They Do and How to Use Them

Most people have heard the word “firewall,” but few understand what it really does—or why it’s absolutely essential for anyone serious about cybersecurity. Whether you’re a solopreneur, a remote worker, or a concerned parent, firewalls are one of your most powerful lines of defense against cyber threats. They’re not just for big corporations or high-tech firms. In fact, if you’re using the internet, you’re already relying on at least one firewall—though it may not be working as hard as it should.

At its core, a firewall is a digital gatekeeper. It monitors incoming and outgoing traffic between your device or network and the internet. Every time your computer tries to send or receive data—whether loading a web page, opening an email, or accessing cloud storage—the firewall checks that data against a set of rules. If something looks suspicious, or if it’s not on the “approved” list, it gets blocked. This process happens in real-time and is the first major line of defense against malware, viruses, hackers, and unauthorized access.

There are three types of firewalls every non-technical user should know about: **software firewalls**, **hardware firewalls**, and **cloud-based firewalls**.

Software firewalls are programs installed directly on your device. Both Windows and macOS come with built-in firewalls that are typically turned on by default. These software-based firewalls filter data on a per-device level. For example, they might block a suspicious app from connecting to the internet or prevent unauthorized remote access to your machine. You can also install third-party firewall software like GlassWire or Little Snitch for more control and better visibility into your network activity. These tools let you see exactly which apps are sending or receiving data, which can be eye-opening.

Hardware firewalls, on the other hand, sit between your internet connection and your device—usually as part of your router. They protect your entire network rather than individual devices. Think of them as the bouncers at the front door of your digital house. If configured correctly, they block malicious traffic before it even reaches your laptop or phone. Many home routers have a basic firewall built in, but higher-end models or business-grade routers offer more advanced firewall settings, like intrusion prevention and geo-blocking. If you run a home business or store client data, upgrading your router to one with a strong firewall can be a wise move.

Cloud-based firewalls, also known as firewall-as-a-service (FWaaS), are growing in popularity for remote teams and digital nomads. These firewalls sit in the cloud and protect your internet connection no matter where you are. You can think of them as VPNs with extra intelligence. Services like NordLayer or Perimeter 81 combine encryption with firewall protection to stop threats before they even reach your local device. This is ideal if you use multiple devices or work in coffee shops and co-working spaces with public Wi-Fi.

So how do you actually use a firewall? First, check your device's settings. On Windows, go to the Control Panel > Windows Defender Firewall. On macOS, go to System Settings > Network > Firewall. Make sure it's turned on. Next, check your router's manual or web interface to verify that the network firewall is active. Most routers allow you to log in using your browser (e.g., 192.168.1.1 or 10.0.0.1) and view the firewall settings. Look for options like SPI (Stateful Packet Inspection), port blocking, and parental controls.

For an extra layer of visibility, install a third-party firewall monitor. Apps like GlassWire give you a dashboard of which apps are sending data and when. If you see something you don't recognize—like a strange IP address communicating with your system—you can block it with one click. This turns your firewall from a passive protector into an active part of your daily security habits.

Now let's talk about ports. Firewalls also manage which ports on your device are open. A port is like a door into your system—some are needed for normal operations, like browsing the web or checking email, but others are potential entry points for hackers. Most firewalls block unnecessary ports by default, but advanced users can customize which ports are open or closed. Unless you're running a server or game network, it's best to leave most ports closed.

Firewalls also offer protection against **DDoS attacks** (distributed denial-of-service), which flood your network with fake traffic to slow it down or crash it entirely. Business-grade firewalls can detect these patterns and block them in real-time. While less common for individuals, these attacks are on the rise—and if you host any kind of online service, you should be prepared.

Finally, firewalls aren't set-it-and-forget-it tools. You should periodically check for updates, adjust rules based on new threats, and review your firewall logs if you notice unusual activity. If you run a business, consider having a simple firewall policy in place that defines what traffic is allowed, what's blocked, and who can make changes.

In the end, firewalls are like digital bodyguards. They quietly work in the background, filtering, blocking, and protecting your data. But with just a little attention from you, they can become far more powerful. And as threats evolve, your firewall should evolve too—because your first line of defense is only strong if it's properly maintained.

Lana's firewall story

A few months after a major data breach rocked her favorite online productivity app, Lana decided it was time to take her digital security seriously. She worked as a virtual assistant for six different clients, juggling everything from emails and calendars to bookkeeping and document storage. While she had always assumed that basic antivirus software and strong passwords were enough, the news of millions of user accounts being compromised made her question everything.

That's when she stumbled across a podcast that explained firewalls in simple terms. It described them as digital bodyguards, quietly standing between your devices and the internet, inspecting all the traffic that comes in and goes out. Intrigued, Lana opened her laptop and checked her settings. The Windows Firewall was already turned on, but she had no idea what it was doing—or if it was even working correctly.

She reached out to her cousin Nate, a software engineer, and asked for help. They got on a Zoom call, and Nate gave her a crash course on firewalls. "Think of your device like a house," he explained. "The firewall is the security gate. It decides who gets in and who stays out. Without it, you're basically leaving your front door open."

Together, they reviewed her Windows firewall settings. It was active, but Nate noticed that a few unnecessary ports were open due to a peer-to-peer app she had installed years ago and forgotten about. He helped her disable it and tighten her firewall rules. Then he asked about her home Wi-Fi router.

"I have whatever came with my internet plan. I never touch it," she said.

Nate shook his head. "That router has a basic firewall, but it's usually weak and outdated. Let's log in and check."

They accessed her router through a browser and discovered that while the firewall was on, key features like SPI filtering and DoS protection were disabled. Worse, the login credentials were still set to the factory default. Lana was stunned. Anyone could have accessed her router with a quick Google search. Nate helped her change the password, enable advanced firewall settings, and turn on parental controls to block known malicious websites.

But he didn't stop there. Nate suggested that because she worked remotely with sensitive client information, she should consider a dedicated firewall device—something like the Firewalla or CUJO AI. Lana hesitated at first, thinking it would be overkill, but when Nate explained that it would allow her to monitor all devices on her home network, including smart TVs and phones, she agreed.

Two days later, her new device arrived. It took less than 30 minutes to install. Instantly, Lana began seeing real-time alerts for unknown devices trying to ping her network. It was unnerving but eye-opening. She now had full visibility into what was happening in her digital environment—something she'd never had before.

Over the next few weeks, Lana developed a new habit. Every Friday morning, before diving into work, she'd check her firewall logs and dashboard. It became part of her routine, just like checking her bank account or reading her email. It gave her peace of mind and a sense of control she'd never felt with technology before.

Later that month, one of her clients reached out in a panic. Their virtual assistant had accidentally downloaded a fake invoice, and their network was now infected. Lana calmly explained the basics of firewalls and walked them through how to check their router settings. They were impressed—and grateful.

Lana realized that firewalls weren't just some techy concept—they were a necessity. And more importantly, they were completely manageable with the right tools and mindset. She didn't have to become a cybersecurity expert. She just had to care enough to take the first step.

What had once seemed invisible and unimportant had now become the foundation of her digital safety. And with every blocked threat and every alert prevented, she felt a little stronger—and a little safer.

Chapter 4: Cloud Storage Security: Dropbox, Google Drive, iCloud & Alternatives

Cloud storage has transformed how we work, communicate, and back up our lives. Whether you're saving family photos, financial documents, client contracts, or creative work, it's likely stored in a cloud platform like Dropbox, Google Drive, or iCloud. But convenience can come at a cost—especially if your cloud storage isn't properly secured. In this chapter, we'll break down how cloud storage works, the risks involved, and the tools and techniques you can use to protect your data from being leaked, stolen, or locked away.

At its simplest, cloud storage means storing your files on remote servers rather than locally on your device. These servers are maintained by companies like Google, Apple, and Microsoft, and you access them through the internet. While this offers incredible benefits—accessing your files from anywhere, syncing across devices, automatic backup—it also creates new vulnerabilities. You're trusting a third party to keep your data secure. And if that trust is broken, your information could be compromised without your knowledge.

Most major cloud storage providers offer **encryption**, both **in**

transit (as your files are uploaded or downloaded) and **at rest** (while sitting on the servers). However, in many cases, these companies retain access to your encryption keys. That means their staff, or hackers who breach their systems, could potentially access your data. This isn't theoretical—cloud services have been hacked before. The infamous iCloud celebrity photo leak was a reminder that even big names with big budgets can be breached.

The solution is to take responsibility for your cloud security. Step one is choosing the right provider. Services like Dropbox, Google Drive, and iCloud are popular for good reason: they're fast, easy to use, and integrate well with your devices. But if you're storing sensitive documents, consider zero-knowledge providers like **Sync.com**, **Tresorit**, or **pCloud**. These platforms ensure that *only you* have the encryption keys. Even the company itself cannot access your files, which means even in the event of a breach, your data remains protected.

If you're committed to using a mainstream provider, you can still boost your protection. Use **file-level encryption** before uploading. Tools like **Cryptomator**, **VeraCrypt**, or **AxCrypt** allow you to encrypt your documents with a password *before* they ever touch the cloud. This creates a double layer of protection. Even if someone gets into your

Dropbox account, they won't be able to open the files without your encryption key.

Next, turn on **two-factor authentication (2FA)** for all your cloud accounts. 2FA requires a second form of identity verification, like a code sent to your phone, to log in. This drastically reduces the chances of someone accessing your account—even if they steal your password. All major platforms support 2FA, but it's often optional, so you'll need to activate it in your account settings.

Be selective about **what you store** in the cloud. Never upload sensitive personal documents—like passport scans, tax returns, or legal contracts—without encrypting them first. Consider what would happen if someone accessed your account. Could they open a credit card in your name? Leak embarrassing personal files? Lock you out of your own work? If the answer is yes, encrypt before uploading or don't upload at all.

Also, review your **sharing settings**. One of the biggest risks in cloud storage is accidental exposure. Maybe you meant to share a file with one client, but you used the "Anyone with the link can view" setting. That link can be passed around endlessly without your knowledge. Always use password-protected sharing and set expiration dates for sensitive links. Regularly audit your shared folders and revoke access to anyone who no longer needs it.

Keep in mind that **cloud storage does not equal backup**. Most services sync your files—meaning if you delete something from your local folder, it disappears from the cloud too. For real backup protection, use services like **Backblaze**, **IDrive**, or **Carbonite** that are designed to store snapshots of your system at regular intervals. That way, if you're hit with ransomware or accidentally delete something important, you can restore a previous version.

For businesses and freelancers handling client data, cloud security is even more critical. You should create a written **data storage policy** outlining where files are stored, who has access, how files are encrypted, and how long data is retained. This not only protects your clients but also reduces your liability in case of a breach. Some industries even have legal requirements (like HIPAA or GDPR) that dictate how data must be stored and protected in the cloud.

Finally, monitor your accounts. Many cloud platforms offer **activity logs** that show who accessed what, when, and from where. Set up alerts for unusual login attempts or file changes. If your account ever gets compromised, these logs can help you identify the damage and respond quickly.

Cloud storage isn't going away. In fact, it's becoming more essential than ever. But with great convenience comes the responsibility to protect yourself. Fortunately, with the right tools—secure platforms, encryption, 2FA, and backup strategies—you can enjoy the benefits of the cloud without the anxiety. Like most cybersecurity practices, cloud security isn't about paranoia—it's about preparation. And when your most important files live online, preparation is everything.

Now, let's talk about Meera's cloud storage story

Meera Patel had always been an organized person. As a freelance graphic designer, her cloud folders were immaculate—sorted by client, date, and deliverables. Everything she created, from brand kits to web graphics, lived in Google Drive. She loved how easy it was to collaborate with clients and share live links instead of sending huge attachments. But one day, that convenience became a vulnerability.

It started when she got a frantic email from a long-term client: "Meera, did you mean to share our entire project folder with a competitor?"

Her heart dropped.

She clicked the link her client included and immediately saw what happened. A folder she had meant to share with limited access was accidentally set to "Anyone with the link can view." That link had made its way to someone else—another designer who was now pitching the same project, using her mockups. The betrayal wasn't just professional—it was digital.

Meera quickly removed access and revoked the link, but the damage was already done. Her client didn't feel safe anymore. And for Meera, that one mistake cost her a five-figure contract and her sense of trust in cloud storage.

After the incident, she took a break from client work and did a full audit of her digital systems. What she discovered shocked her. Many of her most sensitive files—contracts, invoices, scanned IDs, tax forms—were stored in Google Drive without encryption. Some had been shared months ago and were still active. A few didn't even require a login to access.

She began researching alternatives and came across a platform called Sync.com, which claimed to be "zero-knowledge." That meant even the company couldn't access her files. She signed up for a free trial and tested it out. The interface was familiar, but the privacy features gave her more control. She started migrating client contracts and sensitive files to Sync while keeping her collaborative design files in Google Drive.

Next, she implemented file-level encryption. Using a tool called Cryptomator, she began encrypting folders before uploading them anywhere. Now, even if someone stumbled across a shared link, they would only see scrambled data without the key. It gave her peace of mind.

She also reviewed all her cloud accounts. Meera turned on two-factor authentication for Google, Dropbox, and her iCloud email. She downloaded activity logs, looked for odd login attempts, and deleted shared links that were no longer needed. She created a master spreadsheet tracking every file she had shared, when it was shared, and when access was removed.

And just to be safe, she signed up for a backup service—IDrive—that stored automatic versions of her projects in case she was ever hit with ransomware or made another mistake. She no longer relied on cloud sync alone.

A few months later, Meera had rebuilt her confidence—and her business. She created a simple one-page PDF she sent to new clients titled, "How I Protect Your Files." It listed the encryption tools she used, how their information was stored, and how access would be granted and revoked. Clients loved it. One said, "You're the first designer I've worked with who takes data security seriously. It makes me trust you more."

What had once been a disaster had turned into an advantage.

Meera realized that cloud storage was like a digital filing cabinet: useful, but only safe if it had a lock—and if you kept track of who had the keys. It wasn't about abandoning convenience. It was about adding intention. And now, with the right tools and awareness, she could use the cloud with confidence—not fear.

Chapter 5: Threat Detection Tools: Antivirus, SIEM, and More

Cybersecurity is not just about building defenses—it's also about knowing when those defenses have been breached. Threat detection tools act like a security camera system for your digital life. Instead of passively trusting that everything is fine, they actively monitor your devices, networks, and accounts for suspicious activity. This chapter will explain the different types of threat detection tools, how they work, and how you can use them to protect your personal and professional data.

At the most basic level, threat detection tools are designed to identify, alert, and sometimes automatically respond to potential security threats. These threats could be viruses, ransomware, phishing attempts, unauthorized logins, data leaks, or unusual network traffic. The goal is to catch issues early—before they cause real damage. The earlier a threat is detected, the easier and cheaper it is to fix.

The first type of threat detection tool most people are familiar with is **antivirus software**. Modern antivirus programs are more than just virus blockers—they often include malware detection, ransomware protection, phishing filters, and even basic firewall features. Well-known names include Norton,

Bitdefender, McAfee, and Kaspersky. For Mac users, tools like Intego or Malwarebytes are popular. While antivirus is important, it's only one layer of protection. Today's cybercriminals use techniques that can bypass basic antivirus software, which is why additional detection layers are important.

The second type is **endpoint detection and response (EDR)** tools. These go beyond antivirus by monitoring your device in real time for unusual activity—such as programs trying to modify system files, suspicious network connections, or processes that mimic ransomware behavior. Popular EDR solutions for small businesses and freelancers include CrowdStrike Falcon, SentinelOne, and Sophos Intercept X. Even if you're not a tech expert, many EDR tools are designed with simple dashboards and automated protection settings.

For larger operations or those handling sensitive data, **Security Information and Event Management (SIEM)** systems are the gold standard. SIEM tools collect and analyze data from across your network—servers, firewalls, devices, cloud services—and look for patterns that indicate a cyberattack. They can detect things like multiple failed login attempts from unusual locations, mass file deletions, or unauthorized data transfers. While SIEM systems like Splunk, LogRhythm, or IBM QRadar are often used by corporate IT departments, smaller-scale versions like Sumo Logic or AlienVault can be configured for individual consultants or small businesses.

Another important detection tool is **Intrusion Detection Systems (IDS)**, which monitor network traffic for known attack signatures or abnormal patterns. Some IDS tools are passive (they alert you when something is wrong), while others, called **Intrusion Prevention Systems (IPS)**, can automatically block malicious activity. Cloud-based solutions like Cloudflare and network hardware like Ubiquiti's UniFi Security Gateway offer IDS/IPS features that are accessible even to non-technical users.

You should also be aware of **Dark Web monitoring services**. These tools scan dark web forums, marketplaces, and data dumps for your personal information, such as email addresses, passwords, or Social Security numbers. If they find a match, you're alerted so you can change your passwords or take other protective measures. Services like HaveIBeenPwned, Experian IdentityWorks, and Norton LifeLock offer this functionality, and some password managers like Dashlane or 1Password include dark web scanning in their premium plans.

Threat detection is not just about software—it's also about

alert configuration. A detection tool that doesn't notify you in time is practically useless. When setting up your tools, enable real-time notifications for critical events, such as:

- Login from a new device or unusual location
- Multiple failed login attempts
- Large file transfers or deletions
- New app or program installations without your approval

One of the most effective ways to use threat detection tools is through **layering**. For example, you might use antivirus software for basic protection, an EDR tool for advanced device monitoring, and a cloud firewall with IDS/IPS for network protection. This combination covers different entry points, making it much harder for an attacker to slip through unnoticed.

It's important to balance security with usability. Too many alerts can lead to "alert fatigue," where you start ignoring notifications altogether. Customize your settings so you're only notified about high-priority threats. And always review your detection logs weekly, even if you haven't received any alerts. Sometimes, you'll spot patterns—like repeated login attempts from the same IP address—that might warrant action before an actual breach occurs.

Finally, remember that threat detection is not a substitute for prevention. Detection tools tell you when something is wrong; they don't stop all attacks before they happen. They are most effective when combined with strong passwords, encryption, firewalls, and good security habits. Think of them as the alarm system that complements the locks on your doors and windows.

By the end of this chapter, you should see threat detection not as an optional add-on, but as a fundamental part of your cybersecurity toolkit. With the right tools and alert settings, you can turn your devices into proactive defenders—ready to spot and respond to danger before it becomes a crisis.

How Daniel learned to use threat detection tools

Daniel Cho had been running his small IT consulting business for seven years. Most of his work came from helping local shops and freelancers set up networks, troubleshoot software issues, and recover lost files. He prided himself on being fast, affordable, and trustworthy. But one Friday afternoon, a single phone call would force him to rethink his entire approach to cybersecurity.

It was from his biggest client, a law firm that handled sensitive corporate cases. Their managing partner sounded panicked. "Daniel, we can't open any of our case files. We're getting a message saying they're encrypted and we have to pay Bitcoin to get them back."

Daniel's stomach dropped. It was ransomware—he knew the symptoms instantly. He rushed to the office, plugged into their network, and started assessing the damage. The ransomware had spread across multiple workstations and into their shared cloud folders. There was no sign of an alert from their antivirus software. In fact, it seemed like the malware had been sitting quietly for weeks before finally activating.

When Daniel traced the entry point, he discovered that it came from a phishing email a junior paralegal had opened. But what shocked him more was that the firm had no **threat detection tools** beyond a basic antivirus program that hadn't been updated in months. There were no endpoint detection systems, no intrusion alerts, no monitoring of unusual file changes—nothing that could have caught the infection early.

The recovery was painful. Daniel had to restore weeks of work from backups, rebuild systems, and guide the firm through notifying affected clients. The law firm kept him on, but the incident left a mark on his reputation. "If you're our tech guy, why didn't you know this was coming?" one partner asked bluntly.

That question stung. Daniel realized that in focusing on fixing problems, he had neglected preventing them—or even detecting them before they became disasters. He spent the next month learning everything he could about threat detection tools. He signed up for demos of endpoint detection and response (EDR) platforms like CrowdStrike and Sophos Intercept X. He tested dark web monitoring services, set up intrusion detection on his own network, and learned how to configure real-time alerts for suspicious activity.

He also invested in a small-scale **SIEM system**—something he'd previously thought was only for large corporations. The tool collected logs from client devices, routers, and cloud platforms, scanning them for anomalies. Within a week of deployment, the SIEM caught an unusual login attempt to a client's email account from a country they'd never done business with. Daniel contacted the client immediately, reset the password, and enabled two-factor authentication. The client was impressed and grateful, telling Daniel, "You might have just saved me from a breach."

Encouraged, Daniel began offering "Proactive Cybersecurity Monitoring" as a service. He installed EDR tools on client laptops, set up alerts for failed login attempts, and monitored dark web leaks for their email addresses. The response was overwhelmingly positive. Clients who had once seen him as just a "tech fixer" now saw him as a strategic security partner.

Six months later, that same law firm called him again—this time, not with a crisis, but with praise. They'd received multiple suspicious emails over the past week, but their detection tools had flagged them instantly. No one had clicked a single malicious link. Their files were safe, their operations uninterrupted.

Daniel realized that threat detection wasn't just a layer of security—it was the bridge between prevention and response. Without it, you were blind to what was happening in your own systems. With it, you could see danger coming before it knocked on your digital door.

And now, when clients asked him what he did, he didn't say, "I fix computers." He said, "I stop cyberattacks before you even know they're happening."

Chapter 6: Password Managers, 2FA, and Secure Authentication Tools

Strong authentication is one of the most effective ways to protect your accounts, yet it's also one of the most neglected areas of personal and business cybersecurity. Many breaches happen not because hackers are exceptionally skilled, but because users rely on weak, reused, or easily guessed passwords. In this chapter, we'll explore how password managers, two-factor authentication (2FA), and other secure login tools can drastically reduce your risk—without making your digital life harder.

Let's start with the problem: password fatigue. The average internet user has between 80 and 100 online accounts, yet most people reuse the same few passwords across multiple sites. This is dangerous because if one site is breached and your password is leaked, attackers will try that same password on your other accounts in what's called **credential stuffing**. The only true defense is to use a unique, strong password for every account. But memorizing dozens—or hundreds—of unique passwords is impossible without help. That's where **password managers** come in.

A password manager is a secure vault that stores all your login credentials in one encrypted location. You only have to remember a single master password, and the manager takes care of generating and remembering the rest. Popular options include **1Password**, **LastPass**, **Bitwarden**, and **Dashlane**. These tools can generate complex passwords—like @Z5n!q8Rp#L2—that would be nearly impossible to guess or brute-force. The passwords are stored in an encrypted form, and only you have the key to unlock them.

When choosing a password manager, look for one with **zero-knowledge architecture**, meaning even the service provider cannot access your stored passwords. Also consider whether you need features like family or team sharing, emergency access, or integration with multiple devices and browsers. Cloud-synced managers are convenient because they keep your vault updated across devices, but local-only managers (like KeePass) are a good choice for those who want maximum privacy and are willing to manually sync their vault.

Now, even with strong, unique passwords, there's another step you should take: **two-factor authentication (2FA)**. This adds an extra layer of security by requiring a second verification method in addition to your password. Even if someone steals your password, they won't be able to log in without the second factor. Common forms of 2FA include:

- **Authenticator apps** like Google Authenticator,

Authy, or Microsoft Authenticator, which generate time-based codes.

- **Hardware security keys** like YubiKey or Titan Security Key, which are physical devices that plug into your computer or connect wirelessly to your phone.
- **SMS verification codes**, which are better than nothing but less secure because they can be intercepted through SIM-swapping attacks.

Authenticator apps and hardware keys are generally the most secure. Hardware keys, in particular, are almost impossible to phish because they won't work on fake websites. Many businesses now require employees to use hardware keys for accessing sensitive systems.

Another tool worth considering is **single sign-on (SSO)** for business environments. SSO lets users log in once to a central system and gain access to multiple apps without needing separate credentials for each. While SSO reduces password fatigue and simplifies management, it also means that the central login needs extremely strong security—ideally a hardware key and 2FA.

You should also regularly audit your accounts to enable 2FA wherever it's available. Most major platforms—Google, Apple,

Microsoft, Facebook, Instagram, Dropbox—offer it in their settings, but it's often buried under "Security" or "Login Options." Some password managers, like 1Password and Dashlane, can even scan your accounts and tell you which ones support 2FA but haven't been enabled.

When using password managers and authentication tools, follow these best practices:

1. **Choose a strong master password**—make it long, unique, and memorable to you. Avoid anything that can be guessed from your social media or public records.

2. **Back up your 2FA codes**—most authenticator apps allow you to export or back them up to avoid being locked out if your phone is lost or stolen.

3. **Update compromised passwords immediately**—if a breach is reported, use your manager's "password change" function to generate a new one.

4. **Be cautious with shared logins**—use secure sharing features in your manager instead of sending passwords via email or text.

5. **Regularly review your vault**—delete old, unused accounts and ensure all active accounts have unique passwords and 2FA enabled.

The reality is that attackers often go for the lowest-hanging fruit. If you're using weak passwords or reusing the same credentials, you're making their job easy. But by combining a password manager with strong 2FA, you dramatically raise the barrier to entry. Even if your data is exposed in a breach, attackers won't be able to move further without the second factor.

Secure authentication is not just a "tech thing"—it's a personal safety measure, much like locking your front door. It protects not just your money, but also your identity, your reputation, and your privacy. And with modern tools, it's easier than ever to implement without adding stress to your daily routine.

How Sofia learned about password managers

Sofia Alvarez had always considered herself careful online. She didn't click suspicious links, avoided strange emails, and even changed her passwords every few months. But what she didn't realize was that she was making the same mistake millions of others do—reusing variations of the same password for most of her accounts.

It all started with a single breach. One night, while scrolling through her phone, she received a security alert from her email provider: "Suspicious login attempt detected from an unfamiliar location." She changed her password immediately, thinking the problem was solved. But two weeks later, she found charges on her bank account for online purchases she hadn't made. Then her Instagram account was taken over, followed by her freelance portfolio site.

It turned out that when a small online store she had shopped at years ago was hacked, her old password ended up on the dark web. Attackers used it to try logging in to other accounts, and because she used similar passwords everywhere, they had a high success rate.

Shaken, Sofia called her friend Marcus, a cybersecurity consultant, who didn't mince words. "You need a password manager and two-factor authentication—yesterday."

The next day, Marcus sat with her over coffee and walked her through setting up Bitwarden, a secure, open-source password manager. He explained how it could generate long, random passwords for each account and store them in an encrypted vault only she could unlock with a master password. At first, Sofia was skeptical—"What if the manager gets hacked?"—but Marcus explained the zero-knowledge encryption model. Even if the service was compromised, her data would be unreadable without her master key.

They spent hours changing her passwords, starting with her most important accounts: email, banking, and social media. Each got a unique, 20-character password generated by the manager. Then they enabled two-factor authentication (2FA) on every service that supported it. For her email and bank accounts, Marcus recommended a hardware key—a small device she plugged into her laptop or tapped against her phone. For her other accounts, she used the Authy app, which generated time-based codes that expired every 30 seconds.

Within days, Sofia began to feel the difference. She no longer worried about remembering every password—Bitwarden did it for her. She got real-time alerts if a service she used had been breached, and she could change her password with a single click. Logging in took a few extra seconds with 2FA, but she found it oddly reassuring—like double-locking the door at night.

A month later, one of her less important accounts sent her a "data breach" notice. The old Sofia would have panicked. This time, she simply opened her password manager, confirmed that her password for that account was unique and unused elsewhere, and deleted the account entirely. No damage, no stress.

Sofia didn't stop there. She helped her parents set up their own password manager, and she gave a short presentation to her freelance networking group about the dangers of password reuse. She even started including "security checklists" in her onboarding packets for new clients, explaining how she protected shared documents and logins.

What had started as a frightening lesson in cyber vulnerability became a turning point in her digital life. She went from being a target to being resilient. Now, when friends complain about remembering passwords or losing accounts, she smiles and says, "You only need to remember one—the master password. After that, the tools take care of you."

Chapter 7: Incident Response: What to Do When Something Goes Wrong

Even the best cybersecurity strategies cannot guarantee total immunity from attacks. A determined hacker, a careless click, or a clever scam can bypass even the strongest defenses. That's why having a well-thought-out **incident response plan** is as essential as locks and alarms—you hope you never need it, but you'll be grateful it's there if something goes wrong.

An **incident** in cybersecurity terms refers to any event that compromises—or attempts to compromise—the confidentiality, integrity, or availability of your data or systems. This could be a confirmed malware infection, a phishing scam that captured login credentials, ransomware encrypting files, unauthorized access to a cloud account, or even a lost device containing sensitive information. The key to minimizing damage is acting quickly, methodically, and without panic.

A proper incident response plan has **five core phases**: Preparation, Identification, Containment, Eradication, and Recovery. Some organizations add a sixth—Post-Incident Review—to learn from the event and improve future defenses.

1. Preparation

Preparation is everything. This phase is about setting up the tools, policies, and resources you'll need before an incident happens. You should have:

- An up-to-date inventory of devices, accounts, and data storage locations.
- Access to emergency contacts such as IT support, cloud service providers, or legal counsel.
- Backups of critical files stored securely and tested regularly to ensure they can be restored.
- A written incident response checklist to guide you step by step.

Preparation also means training yourself and your team on recognizing suspicious activity and knowing who to alert. If you're a solo business owner or freelancer, it means deciding in advance who you can call for help and how you'll communicate during an incident.

2. Identification

This phase is about recognizing that something is wrong. Indicators can include:

- Unusual account logins from unknown locations.

- Files disappearing or being encrypted without your action.
- Devices slowing down dramatically or behaving erratically.
- Antivirus or threat detection alerts. The faster you identify a potential breach, the more likely you are to contain it before significant damage occurs. Sometimes, detection comes from automated tools like endpoint protection or SIEM systems; other times, it's a human noticing something odd.

3. Containment

Once you know there's a problem, your first priority is to stop the attack from spreading. Depending on the situation, this might mean:

- Disconnecting affected devices from the internet.
- Temporarily suspending user accounts.
- Blocking specific IP addresses or network ports. Containment buys you time to investigate without allowing further damage. For example, if ransomware has infected one computer on a network, unplugging

that machine immediately can prevent it from encrypting shared files.

4. Eradication

After the threat is contained, you need to remove it completely. This could involve:

- Running full malware scans and removing infected files.
- Resetting compromised passwords and enabling 2FA.
- Restoring clean versions of files from backup.
- Applying software patches to close exploited vulnerabilities. It's critical to identify the root cause—whether it was a phishing link, outdated software, or a misconfigured firewall—so you can prevent a repeat.

5. Recovery

Recovery is the process of restoring systems to normal operation. This could mean reinstalling applications, reconnecting devices to the network, or re-enabling suspended accounts. You should also monitor closely for signs that the attacker is trying to regain access. For business owners, this phase often includes notifying clients, partners, or regulators if sensitive data was exposed.

6. Post-Incident Review

Once the crisis has passed, take time to analyze what happened and how well your response worked. Ask yourself:

- How did the attacker get in?
- How long did it take to detect and respond?
- What worked well and what needs improvement? Update your security policies, tools, and training based on these insights. This step ensures that every incident—no matter how small—makes you more prepared for the next one.

Pro Tips for Effective Incident Response:

- Always document the timeline of events, actions taken, and outcomes. This can be crucial for legal purposes or insurance claims.
- Keep a printed copy of your incident response plan in case your digital files are inaccessible.
- Test your plan at least once a year with a simulated incident.

The biggest mistake people make during a cyber incident is hesitating out of uncertainty. The second biggest mistake is overreacting without a plan. An incident response framework gives you confidence and clarity when every second counts. You don't need to be a security expert to have one—you just need to be ready.

Let's talk about Ethan's shocking story

On a chilly Monday morning in February, Ethan Williams walked into his small architectural firm expecting a quiet day. Instead, his receptionist greeted him with panic in her voice. "Ethan, the files on the server... they're gone. All I see are strange names with weird extensions, and there's a note asking for Bitcoin."

Ethan felt a pit in his stomach. He hurried to his office and opened the shared drive. Every project—blueprints, proposals, invoices—was replaced with encrypted files and a ransom note. The message was chilling: *"Your files are locked. Pay within 72 hours or they will be deleted forever."*

He didn't have an IT department, just a part-time tech guy named Trevor who came in once a month to do updates. Ethan called him immediately. Trevor arrived within the hour, took one look, and said, "Ransomware. We need to move fast."

Trevor's first move was **containment**. He unplugged the affected computers from the network, disconnected the Wi-Fi, and locked down the router to prevent the ransomware from spreading to cloud backups or other devices. Ethan's staff looked bewildered, unsure what to do, but Trevor kept his instructions short and calm: "No one touches anything. Don't plug in any drives. Just wait."

Next came **identification**. Trevor began checking logs and tracing the source of the infection. He found it almost immediately: a phishing email disguised as a package delivery notice, opened by an intern on Friday afternoon. The malware had been sitting dormant all weekend before triggering that morning.

Once the threat was isolated, they moved to **eradication**. Trevor ran specialized malware removal tools on the infected systems. It took hours, but eventually, they cleared the ransomware. The files, however, were still encrypted. Thankfully, Trevor had implemented an **offline backup** protocol months earlier—something Ethan had once thought was overkill. That backup, stored on a separate drive disconnected from the network, contained nearly everything except the last two days of work.

Recovery was slow but steady. They restored the clean backup, recreated the few missing files from paper copies, and reset all passwords. Trevor also enabled two-factor authentication on every account and updated every device with the latest patches.

When the immediate crisis ended, Ethan sat in his office and thought about how close they'd come to disaster. Without Trevor's calm, methodical response, they could have lost years of work—or paid a ransom to criminals with no guarantee of getting anything back.

The following week, Trevor held a **post-incident review** with the team. He walked them through what happened, how it was handled, and how to avoid similar attacks. He showed them the phishing email that started it all and explained why it looked suspicious. He also gave them a laminated "Incident Response Quick Guide" with steps to follow if they ever suspected an attack.

Ethan made incident response training a regular part of the firm's schedule. He also invested in better threat detection tools, stronger firewalls, and a business continuity plan. For him, the experience was more than a wake-up call—it was a transformation.

Now, when other small business owners asked about cybersecurity, Ethan didn't hesitate. "You don't have to be an expert," he'd say. "You just need a plan. Because when something goes wrong—and trust me, it will—the difference between a disaster and a close call is how you respond."

Chapter 8: Building a Cybersecurity Toolkit on a Budget

When most people hear the phrase "cybersecurity toolkit," they imagine expensive enterprise-level software and a full-time IT department. But the truth is, you can build a highly effective personal or small business security setup without draining your bank account. This chapter will show you how to assemble the essential tools for protecting your data, devices, and accounts—while keeping costs low or even free.

A **cybersecurity toolkit** is simply a collection of tools and services that work together to prevent, detect, and respond to threats. The exact contents will vary depending on your needs, but a well-rounded kit should cover six key areas: password management, malware protection, network security, data encryption, backup and recovery, and monitoring.

1. Password Management

A strong, unique password for every account is your first line of defense. While paid managers like 1Password and Dashlane offer premium features, free options like **Bitwarden** or **KeePassXC** provide excellent core functionality. They generate and store strong passwords in an encrypted vault, sync across devices, and even alert you if a password appears in a known breach. Choosing a zero-knowledge password manager ensures that only you have the keys to your vault.

2. Malware Protection

You don't need to pay for expensive antivirus software to get solid protection. **Windows Security** (built into Windows 10 and 11) and **XProtect** (built into macOS) are surprisingly robust for basic use. If you want extra features like ransomware protection or web filtering, free versions of **Avast** or **AVG** can be layered on. The key is to keep your antivirus updated and run regular scans.

3. Network Security

Firewalls and secure network setups are essential, but you don't have to invest in enterprise gear. Most home routers include a built-in firewall—just make sure it's enabled. For added security on public Wi-Fi, use a reputable VPN. Services like **Proton VPN** and **Windscribe** offer free plans with limited bandwidth but strong encryption. If you can afford a small upgrade, investing in a higher-quality router like TP-Link or ASUS models with advanced security settings can make a big difference.

4. Data Encryption

Encryption is critical for protecting files and communication. For device-level encryption, use the built-in tools—**BitLocker** for Windows and **FileVault** for macOS—both of which are free. For encrypting specific files or folders before uploading to the cloud, free tools like **VeraCrypt** or **Cryptomator** work well. For encrypted email, try **ProtonMail**'s free tier. For messaging, **Signal** is a free, open-source app that offers end-to-end encryption for texts, calls, and file sharing.

5. Backup and Recovery

A secure backup can mean the difference between minor inconvenience and total disaster after an attack. For free cloud backups, **Google Drive**, **Dropbox Basic**, or **OneDrive** can store essential documents (though always encrypt sensitive files before uploading). For local backups, an external hard drive paired with built-in tools like **Windows Backup** or **Time Machine** costs little upfront but gives long-term peace of mind.

6. Monitoring and Alerts

Many people overlook monitoring tools, but they are vital for spotting threats early. Free dark web scanning services like **HaveIBeenPwned** can alert you if your email or passwords appear in a data breach. Setting up free **Google Alerts** for your business name or personal information can help you spot fraud or impersonation attempts. Some password managers also include free breach monitoring.

Building Your Kit Step-by-Step

If your budget is tight, you can build your toolkit gradually. Start with the essentials—password manager, antivirus, and backups. Then add layers like encryption tools, a VPN, and monitoring services. Remember, cybersecurity is most effective when you use multiple overlapping tools, a concept called **defense-in-depth**.

Keeping Costs Down

To avoid unnecessary expenses:

- Use built-in security features before buying extra software.
- Opt for open-source tools, which are often free and well-reviewed by the security community.
- Take advantage of free tiers of paid services, upgrading only if you truly need the additional features.
- Stay alert for promotions—many premium services offer free months or significant discounts.

Maintenance Matters

Even the best toolkit is useless if it's not maintained. Schedule a monthly security checkup to update software, run scans, review shared file links, and test your backups. Keep your toolkit lean—remove unused tools that could become outdated security risks.

In short, building a cybersecurity toolkit on a budget is entirely possible with the right strategy. By combining built-in protections with carefully chosen free and low-cost tools, you can create a strong security posture that rivals far more expensive setups. You don't need deep pockets—just a plan, consistency, and the discipline to keep your defenses updated.

How Jordan built a cybersecurity toolkit

Jordan Lee had just launched his own photography business, and while he knew how to capture the perfect shot, cybersecurity was not his strong suit. He figured that as long as he had antivirus software and didn't click on suspicious links, he'd be fine. But that assumption was tested one summer afternoon when he received a frantic message from a client: *"Jordan, did you just email me an invoice link? It looks weird and my computer flagged it."*

Jordan hadn't sent anything. A quick check confirmed his worst fear—his email account had been hacked. The attacker had sent malicious links to several clients, damaging his reputation and prompting a wave of concerned calls. He spent hours changing passwords and reassuring customers, but the damage was done.

Determined to never let it happen again, Jordan started researching how to protect himself. At first, the sheer volume of security tools and services overwhelmed him. It all sounded expensive—something big corporations could afford, but not a freelancer trying to pay the bills. But after digging deeper, he discovered a different reality: he could build a **cybersecurity toolkit** for almost nothing if he used the right mix of free and low-cost tools.

He started with a free account on **Bitwarden**, a password manager that let him store all his logins in one secure vault. Gone were the days of reusing weak passwords. He also enabled two-factor authentication on every account that supported it, using **Authy** for generating codes on his phone.

Next, he turned his attention to malware protection. He realized that his Windows laptop already came with **Windows Security**, which, when kept up to date, was strong enough for his needs. He scheduled weekly scans and made a note to keep his operating system updated automatically.

For network security, Jordan checked his home router settings for the first time since he'd moved in. He enabled the built-in firewall, changed the default password, and set up a separate guest network for visitors. When working in cafés or airports, he started connecting through **Proton VPN**'s free plan to encrypt his traffic on public Wi-Fi.

His biggest concern was client data—photos, contracts, and invoices that he often stored in the cloud. Instead of relying solely on his existing Dropbox account, Jordan installed **Cryptomator** to encrypt files before uploading them. This meant that even if someone got into his Dropbox, the files would be unreadable without the encryption key.

For backups, he dusted off an old external hard drive and set up **Windows Backup** to run automatically twice a week. He also kept key project folders synced to his Google Drive, making sure to encrypt sensitive files first.

Finally, Jordan set up a few free monitoring tools. He registered his email addresses on **HaveIBeenPwned** to get alerts if they showed up in a data breach. He also created Google Alerts for his business name to catch any impersonation attempts.

The transformation was immediate—not just in his security posture, but in his confidence. When another client emailed about a suspicious message a month later, Jordan could confidently check his logs, confirm his accounts were secure, and respond within minutes. His toolkit had turned him from reactive to proactive.

A year later, when he gave a talk at a local small business networking event, Jordan shared his story. He passed around a simple checklist of the tools he used—most of them free—and explained how they worked together. Several attendees were surprised that they could protect their businesses without spending thousands.

Jordan realized that cybersecurity wasn't about having the most expensive tools—it was about having the right ones, and using them consistently. And thanks to his budget-friendly toolkit, he could now focus on what he loved most: capturing moments, not cleaning up after cyber incidents.

Chapter 9: Red Flags: Signs You're Being Watched, Hacked, or Tracked

One of the most dangerous aspects of cyber threats is that many people don't know they've been compromised until it's too late. Cybercriminals often operate quietly, gathering information, monitoring activity, and preparing for a larger attack before revealing themselves. The ability to recognize the **red flags** of being watched, hacked, or tracked can mean the difference between stopping an attack early and suffering a costly breach.

1. Unusual Account Activity

Your online accounts—email, banking, social media—are often the first targets for attackers. Warning signs include:

- Login alerts from unfamiliar locations or devices.
- Notifications of password changes you didn't make.
- Emails appearing in your "sent" folder that you didn't send.
- Messages marked as "read" that you haven't opened. Most major platforms allow you to review recent login history. Make it a habit to check these logs and

immediately reset your password (and enable 2FA) if you see anything suspicious.

2. Slow or Erratic Device Performance

While slow performance can be caused by aging hardware or too many open programs, it can also be a sign of malicious software running in the background. Look for:

- Programs opening or closing on their own.
- The mouse cursor moving without your input.
- The hard drive light flickering when you're not actively using your device. These could indicate spyware, remote access tools, or keyloggers capturing your keystrokes. Running a full malware scan with updated antivirus or EDR software can help confirm if your system is clean.

3. Unexpected Pop-Ups or Ads

A sudden increase in pop-ups, browser redirects, or intrusive ads—even when you're not online—can be a sign that your device is infected with adware or more serious malware. Be especially cautious if you see security warnings urging you to "call tech support" or download "urgent updates." These are often scams designed to trick you into installing malicious software or revealing personal information.

4. Battery and Data Drain on Mobile Devices

If your smartphone battery drains unusually fast or your mobile data usage spikes without explanation, it could mean spyware is running in the background. Spyware often transmits data—like location, text messages, and call logs—to a remote server, consuming both power and bandwidth. You can check battery and data usage in your phone's settings to spot apps using more than they should.

5. Changes to Security Settings

Attackers sometimes disable firewalls, antivirus software, or security updates to make future attacks easier. If you notice that protective features are turned off and you didn't change them, treat it as an urgent red flag. Immediately re-enable them, run a malware scan, and consider restoring from a known clean backup.

6. Unexplained Charges or Financial Activity

Cybercriminals often test stolen credit card or banking information with small, inconspicuous charges before making larger withdrawals or purchases. Monitor your financial statements regularly for even the smallest unfamiliar transactions, and report them immediately. For extra protection, set up account alerts to notify you of any activity over a certain amount.

7. Emails or Messages from Services You Don't Use

If you start receiving account verification emails from companies you've never interacted with, it could mean someone is using your email address to register accounts. Similarly, if friends receive suspicious messages from you, your account may already be compromised.

8. Physical Signs of Tampering

For those in sensitive roles, physical evidence—like screws missing from your laptop casing, unfamiliar USB devices plugged in, or changes to your router placement—can indicate someone has tried to access your equipment directly.

What to Do If You See Red Flags

The moment you suspect you're being watched or hacked, take immediate action:

1. Disconnect from the internet to stop ongoing communication between your device and the attacker.

2. Run a full antivirus or EDR scan to detect and remove malicious software.

3. Change your passwords from a clean device, and enable two-factor authentication.

4. Review account activity logs and revoke access from unknown devices.

5. If sensitive data was exposed, consider contacting your bank, credit bureaus, or law enforcement.

Prevention Is Still the Best Defense

While recognizing red flags is crucial, the ultimate goal is to prevent these situations from occurring in the first place. Keep your software updated, avoid downloading apps from unverified sources, and use layered security measures like firewalls, encryption, and threat detection tools.

By learning to spot the subtle signs of compromise, you can act quickly—often before serious damage is done. In cybersecurity, early detection isn't just helpful; it's often the single most important factor in protecting yourself.

Now, lets talk about an unusual story

Angela Morris thought she had a quiet week ahead. As a remote project coordinator, her days were usually predictable—managing spreadsheets, sending emails, and checking in with her team. But on Tuesday morning, something strange happened. Her email notified her of a login from a device in Singapore. She had never been to Singapore.

She brushed it off, thinking it was a glitch, and went back to work. But later that day, she noticed something else odd: several of her sent emails were addressed to people she didn't know, with vague subject lines like *"Important Update"* and *"Please Read Immediately."* She hadn't written them.

The following day, her laptop seemed sluggish. Apps froze unexpectedly, and her cursor occasionally moved on its own for a second before snapping back. She told herself it was probably just a software update running in the background, but deep down, she felt uneasy.

That evening, while paying a few bills online, she saw a $9.73 charge on her bank account from a company she'd never heard of. It was small enough to ignore, but she remembered reading that cybercriminals often test stolen cards with tiny charges before making bigger purchases. Now she was alarmed.

She called her friend Jason, who worked in IT security. After hearing the list of oddities, he said bluntly, "Angela, you're probably compromised. That login from Singapore? That's not a glitch. The weird sent emails? Someone's using your account. The lagging laptop? Could be spyware. You need to act now."

Following Jason's instructions, Angela disconnected from the internet immediately. She used her tablet—one she rarely used for work—to change all her passwords, starting with email, banking, and cloud storage. She enabled two-factor authentication on every account. Then she ran a full malware scan on her laptop, which revealed two pieces of spyware hiding in the system.

Jason helped her wipe the infected files and walked her through reviewing her account activity logs. They found that her attacker had logged in multiple times over the past month, sending spam and likely monitoring her activity. The small bank charge had been the first sign of their financial intentions.

Angela also checked her phone and was shocked to see that her battery usage had been unusually high for the past few weeks, even when she barely used it. Jason suspected a malicious app could have been tracking her location and data. She deleted every app she didn't recognize and updated her phone's operating system.

By the weekend, Angela's devices were clean, and her accounts were secure. But the experience changed her habits forever. She started checking her account logins weekly, monitoring her financial transactions daily, and keeping her security software updated religiously.

A month later, when a coworker mentioned that their email had been acting strangely, Angela immediately recognized the signs and urged them to check their logs and passwords before it got worse.

She realized that cyberattacks often start quietly, with subtle clues that are easy to ignore. But those small red flags—a strange login alert, a mysterious bank charge, an unusual spike in battery usage—are often the only warning you get before the damage escalates. Now, Angela knew to listen to them.

Chapter 10: Creating Your Personal Cyber Defense Plan

Cybersecurity can feel overwhelming when you look at all the possible threats—hackers, phishing scams, ransomware, spyware, data breaches, identity theft. But the truth is, you don't need to be a cybersecurity expert to protect yourself effectively. What you *do* need is a **personal cyber defense plan**—a clear, organized set of steps and tools that you consistently follow to reduce your risks.

Think of your personal cyber defense plan as your own custom-built security system. It's not a single tool or setting; it's a layered approach combining habits, technology, and response strategies. The goal is to make it as difficult and costly as possible for an attacker to succeed while making it easy for you to recover if something does go wrong.

Step 1: Identify Your Risks and Priorities

Before you can design your defense, you need to know what you're protecting and what the biggest threats are. Start by listing:

- The devices you use (laptop, smartphone, tablet, smart home devices).

- The accounts you rely on (email, banking, work platforms, cloud storage).
- The sensitive data you store (financial records, personal documents, client files). Once you know what's at stake, consider the most likely attack scenarios. For example, a small business owner may be more concerned about ransomware and client data breaches, while a frequent traveler might focus on securing devices and using VPNs on public Wi-Fi.

Step 2: Build Your Protection Layers

Your plan should follow the principle of **defense-in-depth**—multiple overlapping protections so that if one layer fails, others still stand. The key layers include:

- **Password security**: Use a password manager and unique, strong passwords for every account. Enable 2FA wherever possible.
- **Device security**: Turn on full-disk encryption (BitLocker for Windows, FileVault for Mac), keep your operating system updated, and run reputable antivirus or EDR software.
- **Network security**: Use a firewall (built-in or hardware) and a VPN on public networks.

- **Data protection**: Encrypt sensitive files and use secure, zero-knowledge cloud storage.
- **Backup strategy**: Maintain at least one offline backup of critical files in addition to cloud backups. Follow the 3-2-1 rule—three copies of your data, stored on two types of media, with one kept offline.

Step 3: Establish Monitoring and Alerts

Many breaches go unnoticed for weeks or months. Set up systems to notify you early:

- Enable login alerts for all major accounts.
- Use services like HaveIBeenPwned to check if your information appears in a breach.
- Review account and device logs weekly for suspicious activity.
- Monitor your credit report and bank accounts for unusual transactions.

Step 4: Plan Your Incident Response

Your plan should clearly outline what you'll do if you suspect a breach:

1. Disconnect the affected device from the internet.
2. Use a clean device to change passwords for critical accounts.
3. Run full malware scans and remove any infections.
4. Restore clean backups if necessary.
5. Contact your bank, credit card companies, or relevant services if financial data is involved.
6. Document what happened and update your plan to prevent a repeat.

Step 5: Train Yourself (and Your Team, if Applicable)

Cybersecurity is as much about behavior as it is about technology. Make it a habit to:

- Pause before clicking on links or opening attachments.
- Verify requests for sensitive information through a second channel (like a phone call).
- Regularly review security settings on devices, apps, and accounts. If you work with a team, schedule short training sessions to keep everyone aware of current threats and prevention methods.

Step 6: Review and Update Regularly

Technology changes quickly, and so do cyber threats. Review your cyber defense plan at least twice a year:

- Update software and replace outdated tools.
- Rotate passwords for critical accounts.
- Adjust your priorities if your situation changes (new job, travel, new devices).

A personal cyber defense plan isn't about being paranoid—it's about being prepared. When you have your defenses mapped out in writing, you're far less likely to be caught off guard. And because you've already decided in advance how to respond, you can act quickly and effectively during an incident, reducing the impact on your data, finances, and peace of mind.

The best defense isn't the most expensive—it's the one you actually use consistently. Your cyber defense plan should fit your lifestyle, budget, and risk level, giving you confidence that you're protected every day, not just when you remember to think about security.

Now, lets go over Melissa's cybersecurity plan

When Melissa Grant's freelance consulting business started to grow, she knew she needed to get serious about her online presence. She was juggling contracts, client data, payment accounts, and dozens of online services. But like many busy professionals, her approach to cybersecurity was inconsistent—she updated her passwords "when she remembered" and kept important documents scattered between her laptop, cloud storage, and email attachments.

Her wake-up call came when a client emailed her, asking why she had sent them an invoice for $4,800 when the actual amount owed was $480. Melissa hadn't sent any invoice that day. She logged into her email and found it filled with bounce-backs from addresses she didn't recognize. Someone had gotten into her account, sent fraudulent invoices to her clients, and was likely trying to redirect payments.

Panic set in, but once she regained control of her email, she decided she would never be caught unprepared again. That weekend, she sat down with a notebook and began mapping out what she called her **Personal Cyber Defense Plan**—a step-by-step guide to protecting every part of her digital life.

The first thing she did was **identify her risks and priorities**. She made a list of every device she used, every account that held sensitive information, and every location where important files were stored. It was eye-opening—there were more accounts and devices to protect than she had realized.

Next, she **built her protection layers**. She subscribed to a password manager and generated unique, strong passwords for every account, enabling two-factor authentication wherever possible. She turned on full-disk encryption for her laptop, updated her antivirus software, and installed a firewall on her router. For public Wi-Fi, she set up a VPN so she could safely work from cafés and airports without worrying about hackers spying on her traffic.

She also created a **monitoring and alerts system**. She set up login notifications for her banking and email accounts, registered her email addresses with HaveIBeenPwned to get breach alerts, and began reviewing her financial transactions every morning before starting work.

Melissa didn't stop at prevention—she mapped out her **incident response plan**. If she suspected a breach, she would immediately disconnect from the internet, switch to a clean backup device, change her passwords, run a full malware scan, and notify clients if their information was at risk. She even printed a one-page "emergency checklist" and taped it to the wall near her desk so she wouldn't lose precious time in a crisis.

She also recognized that her own behavior was a key factor. She trained herself to hover over links before clicking, verify payment requests through a second channel, and pause before downloading attachments. Once a quarter, she scheduled a "security day" to update her software, rotate critical passwords, and check her backups.

Six months later, her plan was put to the test. She received an alert that someone had tried to log into her cloud storage from another country. Instead of panicking, she followed her checklist: changed her password from her backup laptop, enabled additional security verification, and reviewed the account's activity log. Because she had acted quickly, the intruder got nothing.

Looking back, Melissa realized that her cyber defense plan gave her more than just protection—it gave her confidence. She no longer felt like she was reacting to threats in the dark. She had a system, she knew how to use it, and she knew that if something went wrong, she could respond calmly and effectively.

When she spoke at a local business networking event, she shared her story and encouraged others to create their own plans. "You don't need to be a tech expert," she told them. "You just need to think ahead. Because in cybersecurity, the best time to prepare is before anything happens—the second best time is right now."

Epilogue: From Awareness to Action

When you first opened this book, you may have thought of cybersecurity as something distant—something for IT departments, government agencies, or tech-savvy professionals in dark server rooms. But by now, you know the truth: cybersecurity is for everyone. It's for the freelancer sending invoices from a coffee shop, the small business owner managing client records, the parent storing family photos in the cloud, and the traveler connecting to hotel Wi-Fi. If you use the internet—and we all do—you are part of the cybersecurity conversation, whether you want to be or not.

We've covered a lot of ground together. You've learned that **advanced** cybersecurity doesn't mean complicated; it means intentional. You've explored encryption, firewalls, secure cloud storage, threat detection tools, password management, and incident response planning. You've seen how ordinary people—just like you—have faced real threats and turned those moments into turning points. Each chapter has shown that the right mix of tools, habits, and awareness can dramatically reduce your risk without requiring you to become a full-time security expert.

The most important takeaway is that cybersecurity is not a one-time project. It's a **practice**—a set of ongoing habits that become part of your daily and weekly routines. Updating your software, checking account logs, backing up your data, and reviewing your defenses are no different than locking your doors at night or checking your smoke alarms. They're small actions that make a big difference over time.

It's also important to remember that you're not powerless in this fight. Cybercrime thrives on easy targets—people using weak passwords, outdated software, unprotected networks, and poor backup habits. By applying even a few of the strategies in this book, you move yourself out of that "easy target" category. You don't have to be impossible to hack; you just have to be more secure than the next potential victim.

Your **personal cyber defense plan** is the anchor that will keep you steady in an unpredictable digital world. Whether you wrote yours down as we went along or are only now ready to start, the key is to keep it simple, practical, and actionable. Layer your protections. Enable alerts. Encrypt what matters most. And always know how you'll respond when—not if—a suspicious event occurs.

Cybersecurity also has a ripple effect. When you protect yourself, you protect your clients, colleagues, friends, and family. A secure network at home keeps hackers from using your devices to attack others. A properly encrypted client document protects their reputation and business. A simple conversation about two-factor authentication can save someone you know from losing their savings to a phishing scam. You become part of the solution.

As technology evolves, so will cyber threats. Artificial intelligence will make some attacks more convincing and harder to detect. The number of connected devices in our homes and workplaces will continue to grow, each one a potential entry point. Regulations and privacy laws will shift. The landscape will keep changing—but the core principles you've learned here will remain the same: awareness, prevention, detection, and response.

So, where do you go from here? Start with one thing. Maybe it's setting up a password manager. Maybe it's encrypting your phone. Maybe it's drafting a basic incident response checklist. Small steps compound into big protection. You don't have to overhaul your digital life overnight—you just have to start.

One day, you may look back on this moment as the point where you went from a passive internet user to an active defender of your own digital life. And if you share what you've learned with others, you'll amplify that impact. Cybersecurity isn't just about protecting data—it's about protecting people, relationships, opportunities, and trust.

Your digital world is worth defending. Now you have the tools, the knowledge, and the plan. The next step is yours.

www.ingramcontent.com/pod-product-compliance
Lightning Source LLC
LaVergne TN
LVHW022020200926
848481LV00007B/2458